A Trail of Paint

Anjali Raghbeer

illustrated by Soumya Menon

Tulika

"Hurry up Biswajeet!" said Mashi. "Stop playing with your food and let's go."

"But Mashi…" began Biswajeet. Another art gallery? His aunt would get busy buying and selling paintings and sculptures, and what was he supposed to do?

"No. No. No. You can't stay behind," said Mashi. "Besides, this is a Jamini Roy exhibition." She went on, grumbling, "No culture you children have. Do you even know that he is one of our greatest painters?"

Biswajeet mumbled a maybe-yes-maybe-no.

"TV. TV. TV!" said Mashi. "That's all you kids care about."

There was some truth to that. Biswajeet was going to miss his favourite show. He gave a huge yawn and tried to look exhausted, but Mashi's jaw set as she marched out. Just in time Biswajeet grabbed his brand new digital camera, a present from Mashi. At least he wouldn't get bored.

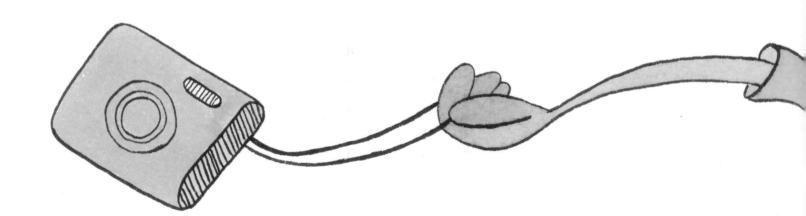

The riksha halted outside the bazaar. Mashi and Biswajeet picked their way through the narrow road and arrived at a freshly painted green door. Over it hung a board that said: GALLERY 55, 55 Naya Bazaar. A lady in a green-and-white cotton sari and a big red bindi rushed up to them.

"Madhulika Sen?" she said. "So glad you could come. I'm Paro. We talked on the phone."

"Paro! You must be so proud of this show," said Mashi. She took a deep breath. "Jamini Roy. A true artist."

"Absolutely. Created his own style." But then Paro frowned. "Mind you, these days you can't be sure which is a real Jamini Roy painting. There are so many fakes floating around."

Biswajeet's eyes grew wide. Fakes?

Mashi nodded in sympathy.

"We, of course, have taken pains to make sure we're displaying only his originals," said Paro. "Everything here is vintage Roy, a hundred per cent."

"But tell me…" said Mashi, following Paro towards the office. She turned to add quickly, "Biswajeet, I'll be a while so just have a look around, will you?" Biswajeet groaned. Typically Mashi — drag him along and then forget about him till her work was done.

He looked around. It was a room with white walls and pictures hung in straight lines. He walked up to one of them. The text on the wall read 'Pujarin', and over it hung a painting of a woman in a blue sari with large almond eyes, carrying a decorated puja thaali.

"A Santhal woman," someone whispered in his ear.

Biswajeet looked around to see a frail old man.

"The artist's favourite subject," said the man.
"Women from the Santhal tribe."

Biswajeet hurried away from him. Why was the man
staring at the painting like that?

He looked around the gallery. There were lots more
Santhal women in different poses. And paintings of
landscapes.

"Creating," the old man whispered again.

"What?" asked Biswajeet. This time the man was studying a bright blue painting of a cat eating a lobster. He shook his head sadly.

"True art," the man said, and suddenly he wasn't whispering any more, "is creating, not copying."

What was he talking about?

Biswajeet peered closer at the painting of the cat and the lobster. But it looked like any other painting to him.

"Here, look at it with this," said the old man, thrusting a magnifying glass into his hands.

Biswajeet looked.

"See the yellow paint?" said the man. "It's so smooth."

"So?" said Biswajeet. What was so great about that?

"That smooth paint is fresh," said the man softly. "Old yellow paint can never look like that. Look here," the man pointed to a painting of Krishna. "See the difference?" he asked.

"The yellow?" Biswajeet squinted, studying the painting.

"Doesn't it look like grains of rice?"

"You're right," said Biswajeet as he magnified the uneven grains of yellow in the Krishna painting.

"You mean the one with the cat is a…" Biswajeet couldn't believe his ears.

"Fake," whispered the old man. His body trembled. His eyes grew watery. He stumbled as he steadied his wispy frame.

"We must tell Paro," said Biswajeet.

"We need proof," the man replied.

Biswajeet shook the old man's hand by the elbow.

"We have to do something, Dadu," cried Biswajeet. "If only we could find the faker. Then Paro will have to believe us."

Dadu looked at Biswajeet.

"Do you know who it is?" Biswajeet urged. "Do you know where he is? Come on, we have to catch him!"

"I don't know if he'll be there now," said Dadu.

That was enough for Biswajeet. He dragged Dadu out of the gallery.

Dadu and Biswajeet rattled their way through Kolkata's Naya Bazaar in a riksha.

Many streets later Dadu said to the rikshawala, "Stop. Here, at the restaurant."

Biswajeet had never been this side before. Everything looked run-down.
"Let's find him quickly and go," he said, feeling a little scared for the first time.

"See that house," said Dadu, pointing to a shabby building. "He comes there every day around lunchtime. I'll keep a watch on it."

Dadu entered the small restaurant and took a window seat. They could easily see the house from there.

The aroma of fried ilish fish wafted through the air.

"Lunch." Biswajeet rubbed his stomach.

"Their ilish is the best in Kolkata," said Dadu, ordering it for both of them.

Biswajeet ate greedily. But Dadu left his food untouched, glancing uneasily out of the window every now and then.

"He's gone in," said Dadu suddenly and rushed out.

He hadn't paid the bill! Biswajeet quickly pulled out some money Mashi had given him and ran out behind Dadu.

"Here, climb on my back and look inside," said Dadu as they reached under a window.

Biswajeet eased himself up, peered in … and froze in shock!

The room was full of paintings just like the ones he had seen at Gallery 55, including an exact replica of 'Pujarin'!

A man with a palette in hand was busy working on a painting.

Biswajeet whipped out his digicam and clicked.

"Dadu, come on," he threw back as he barged into the house.

"Why are you copying?" yelled Biswajeet,
bursting into the room full of paintings.

"Who are you? Go away!" the man snarled.

"True art is about creating…" Biswajeet shouted
back angrily, remembering what Dadu had said.

Dadu stepped in.

"Abhijit, I never thought… You?" Dadu said quietly.

The man's face went pale as he saw Dadu.
His palette dropped. The paint splattered onto the
finished paintings. He fled.

"He's running like he's seen a ghost!" said Biswajeet.

Dadu smiled. "Where will he hide? He's been caught
on camera."

Sitting down suddenly, his shoulders sagging even more, Dadu said sadly, "A man dares to create a style of his own and see what people do."

Biswajeet was quiet.

"These are copies from early works." Dadu pointed to the landscapes and portraits. "At that time he painted like the Europeans."

In spite of being fake, the landscapes transported Biswajeet to the seaside.

"After that he used sweeping brush strokes and brilliant colours … yellows, indigos, vermilions … inspired by the folk people around him."

Dadu's voice trailed off while Biswajeet stared at the indigo of the woman's sari in the painting 'Three Sisters', drowning in its depth.

"He created a style of his own," murmured Dadu.

"Mashi said so too. That he was a true artist," said Biswajeet.

Biswajeet picked up 'Cat Eating a Lobster' and some of the other finished paintings and clicked some more photos. "Mashi will have to do something about this," he said.

"You'd better get back to your Mashi," said Dadu. "It's late."

"And you?" asked Biswajeet.

"I'll wait here till you send someone from the gallery," said Dadu.

The riksha ride back seemed to take forever. As soon as they reached, Biswajeet rushed into the gallery shouting, "MASHI, LOOK!"

Mashi and Paro came running out of the office.

Biswajeet waved his arms at the 'Cat Eating a Lobster' hanging on the wall.

"See! An exact copy!" he unfurled his roll of paintings.

"What … where did you find these?" Paro said, barely audible.

"There are more in that house. Dadu is waiting there. I took pictures," said Biswajeet, scribbling down the address.

A few quick calls and the gallery was swarming with police, art experts and newspaper reporters. Paro and Mashi stood in the centre of all the confusion, still dazed.

Biswajeet went back to the hall with the paintings. It was quiet in there. And then he saw Dadu walk in.

"Did the police come to the house? Did they catch the copier?" Biswajit wanted to know.

"They will, they will," said Dadu, looking at the paintings again.

"Dadu, can I take a picture of you?" asked Biswajeet.

"How about here?" Dadu stood in front of a painting.

Biswajeet focused with his digicam but the picture was hazy. He could see just a white light.

He zoomed his camera lens a little more and in the camera frame he saw only a painting.

"Dadu?" Biswajeet looked around.

He stepped closer to the painting. It was Dadu!

And underneath was written, 'Self-portrait: Jamini Roy.'

SELF-PORTRAIT
JAMINI ROY

Looking at Jamini Roy's paintings

Jamini Roy was born in 1887 and lived in Beliator, a little village in the Bankura district of West Bengal that was famous for its folk art. He spent all his time with the folk artists, called patuas, because he was fascinated by the shapes they drew and the colours they used. He too wanted to be an artist.

So when he was 16 he went to study art in Kolkata. In those days art colleges mainly taught Western methods of painting, and that's what Jamini Roy learnt. The paintings on the left are done in that style. After that, he earned money by painting people's portraits. But his dream was to create his own style, something unique.

He began to experiment. He tried doing sceneries, first in delicate watercolours, and later like the European artists Cezanne and Van Gogh. Then one day he noticed the simple, bold lines of the folk paintings, called pat, sold outside the Kalighat temple in Kolkata – and suddenly, he knew what to do! He had to try painting in the style of folk and tribal artists.

He went back to his village and sat with the patuas once again, watching and learning their technique. He put aside his expensive European paints and used the colours they did, made with natural materials like earth, vegetables, lamp black, chalk powder and leaves. Instead of canvas he painted on cloth, wood, or mats coated with lime.

Slowly, he came up with a clear style. It was inspired by popular Bengali folk art and the paintings of the Santhal tribals who lived around him, yet it was distinctly different. It had bold, simple lines, vibrant colours and sweeping strokes. He called it the flat technique, not like anything he had learnt and practised so far. It was indeed unique.

It took a while before people realised the value of Jamini Roy's art, and he went through many years of hardship. It is said he wouldn't spend more than 50 paise on any painting he made. Even in those days, this was not a lot of money.

Many of his paintings look almost the same. This is because he always saw himself as just a simple patua – his work was to paint, and he was happy to make the same painting over and over again for all who wanted it. This is also why it is difficult to fix a date on his paintings, for there may be similar ones painted at different times.

Jamini Roy dared to be different, to move away from what was considered 'good art' in his time. It took great courage, yet he was always clear about what he wanted – to create a style that was close to his roots, but could be recognised as his own. That, he believed, was true art.

The sketch on the left by Jamini Roy appeared in a magazine in 1948. Interestingly, it looks as if the painting of the drummers below is based on that. Artists often work like this – they first do a rough drawing and then the final painting.

The two pictures in the box on the facing page are traditional pat paintings. In fact, if you look at Jamini Roy's paintings alongside the pats, you will see how he was inspired by this kind of folk art – in the way the feet are crossed and the posture of the body. It is also clear how his art is distinctively different. This shows how beautifully he adapted that style but created his own.

To Pankaj, who embodies the qualities of honesty and integrity – AR

The Looking at Art series:
A Tree in my Village – *Paritosh Sen, painter*
My Name is Amrita – *Amrita Sher-Gil, painter*
A Trail of Paint – *Jamini Roy, painter*
The Veena Player – *Ravi Varma, painter*
Barefoot Husain – *M. F. Husain, painter*
Stitching Stories – *Gujarati folk embroidery*
The Little Clay Horse – *Sonabai Rajawar, terracotta sculptor (forthcoming)*

A Trail of Paint (English)

ISBN 978-81-8146-651-8
© *story* Anjali Raghbeer
© *illustrations* Tulika Publishers
First published in India, 2009
Reprinted in 2011

Design: Radhika Menon

Our deepest thanks to the family of Jamini Roy for permission to reproduce pictures of his paintings for this book, and in particular to Ashoke Roy for all his warm support, patience and cooperation.

Published by
Tulika Publishers, 13 Prithvi Avenue First Street, Abhiramapuram, Chennai 600 018, India
email tulikabooks@vsnl.com website www.tulikabooks.com

Printed and bound by
Sudarsan Graphics, 27 Neelakanta Mehta Street, T. Nagar, Chennai 600 017, India

To order books visit www.tulikabooks.com